Izzy iS Me

Adventures in Autism

Vincent Michael dela Luna

Tellwell Talent
www.tellwell.ca

ISBN
978-0-2288-2964-5 (Hardcover)
978-0-2288-2963-8 (Paperback)
978-0-2288-4676-5 (eBook)

Acknowledgements and Dedication

As this is an acknowledgement, I must start by acknowledging my complete ignorance in the world and struggles of mental health. I thought I knew things and quickly realized that I knew so very little and that what I did know was mostly from inaccurate movies I had watched. I discovered that I had to very quickly learn about life from scratch, sometime in my late thirties.

I learned about autism from medical and social service providers in British Columbia and Hawaii, who have the difficult task of introducing parents to a future world of struggles, difficulty, and the need for self-advocacy.

I learned to better recognize and understand autism from organizations like Monarch House in British Columbia and 'Imi Ola Autism Services in Hawaii.

I learned about patience, love, and 'Ohana (family) from people like Keola Awana and Justine Tubana from 'Imi Ola Autism Services, and Ofelia Reed, Mary Stephany and Sue Lally from Iroquois Point Elementary in Ewa Beach, for in them I saw human beings who willingly chose to go far out of their way to help children they didn't know with difficult and painful struggles.

I learned about kindness and hope from people like Alba Esposito-Brady, Sylvia Ferretti, Alexis Gelowitz, and Brianne Corcoran from St. John Bosco Elementary in Edmonton; they are from the only school in Alberta, of the thirty-six I had scouted, that asked about my children first and then told me how they could help, rather than provide me with excuses for why they couldn't.

I learned about compassion from the dozens of people who chose to give so much of their lives to help others, like Mandi Pineda, Eli Cumplido, Leanne Teves, Teresa Rascon, Joanne Green, Alene Sandry, Carol Marie Kaneshiro, George Judson, Joyce Uyehara, Shaylin Doane-Villiarimo, and all those aides and teachers like Paula Keliinui, Alanna Boyes, Teresa Skinner, Anam Shuaib, Gillian Robertson, Jennifer Johnston and Clair McLeod who were there to help along the way. And of course, my good friend, Karen Lo, who helped for so long with the kids as we built a home in Hawaii.

I learned about unconditional love from my mother and father and two sisters.

I learned about forever from my wife.

I learned about happiness from my kids.

And because of all that I have been able to learn, preparing me for a life of adventures with Nic and Izzy, I dedicate this book to all of you.

My name is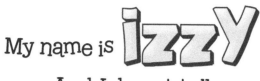

And I do not talk

I have something called autism

But I am sharp as a hawk

I see all things around me

Even things you keep hidden

And when you're not looking

I'll

over and get them

I love all things paper

I like plastic and shoes

They are things I can

Or **bend** and **break**

into two

I tap them

Just outside of my ear

People think I don't listen

But every whisper I hear

I love my routines

And knowing what to expect

So when plans end up changing

I turn into a

Sometimes I understand you

Other times it's confusing

I feel frustrated and

I may cry, so amuse me!

I love feeling the **wind**

And you can calm me

with **bubbles**

Bath time is awesome

Until I make trouble

Water always overflows

To the floor from the tub

My mom sighs, "Oh, Izzy..."

I reply, "Blub blub blub"

jumping

is my favourite

Or maybe it's

running

No, I think it's my dad

And the fun that is coming

He throws me up **high**

Then he spins me around

I laugh when he

tickles

As we roll on the ground

He **sings** to me always

So I know what to do

Sometimes I can sing along

With my own word or two

I learn most things differently

It's quite hard, it's true

But repeating can help

With a  from you

It can feel

overwhelming

When you can't talk to others

I am lucky that I have

Such an awesome big brother

His name is **nic**

He has autism too

And he always protects me

So I'll never feel **blue**

I love to chase others

And love them

chasing me

But loud sounds

can be **scary**

So no **yelling** please

I also like **smelling**

Even big people toes

And I **laugh** when I **fart**

Because I have a nose

balloons

make me happy

And lots of bottles of water

I sort them by shape

And by size and

by colour

My classmates are

They always wave, "Hi"

They are patient and curious

And feel sad when I

Some try to talk to me

I reply with a

Because I sound like a tiger

Then I  and I snort

Playing with sand makes me giggle

Especially at the beach

But I don't understand danger

So I'm always within reach

Of my mommy and daddy

Who **love** me

and my brother

And love all of our

autism

Even when it's a bother

My family calls me Izzy

They help me be all I can be

Autism makes me

But Izzy is me

About the Author

Vincent Michael dela Luna was born on June 9, 1975 in Manila, Philippines. His father, Antonio, and mother, Maria, moved the family to Hamilton, Ontario, Canada in 1977 with little more than the clothes on their backs. Vince has two younger sisters, Antonette and Jennifer.

As Vince grew older, his life took him on his own adventures. He spent time in Rome, London, Toronto, Vancouver, Manila and Honolulu. Vince then returned to Canada to live in Edmonton where he decided to publish his first book.

During a twenty-year span living in Vancouver, British Columbia, Canada, where he made movies and television shows, he met and married his wife, Chix, and assisted in the creation of his two most favourite people, Nic and Izzy. It was also in Vancouver, where Nic and then Izzy were both diagnosed with autism. After years of watching his children grow on opposite sides of the autism spectrum and with Izzy's struggles increasing due to the severity of being non-verbal, Vincent recognized the need to stop working in film and start caring for his children full time.

As Nic and Izzy went about their own adventures, they taught their father the meaning of patience, love, and understanding, and showed him the need for everyone to better understand autism, not just to rid the world of the fear and stigma of it, but simply to help everyone become better and kinder human beings.

And so, begins his first story, designed for children, to try and answer some of their endless questions about Izzy and her autism and why she does what she does.

"be kind to one another"

–Ellen DeGeneres

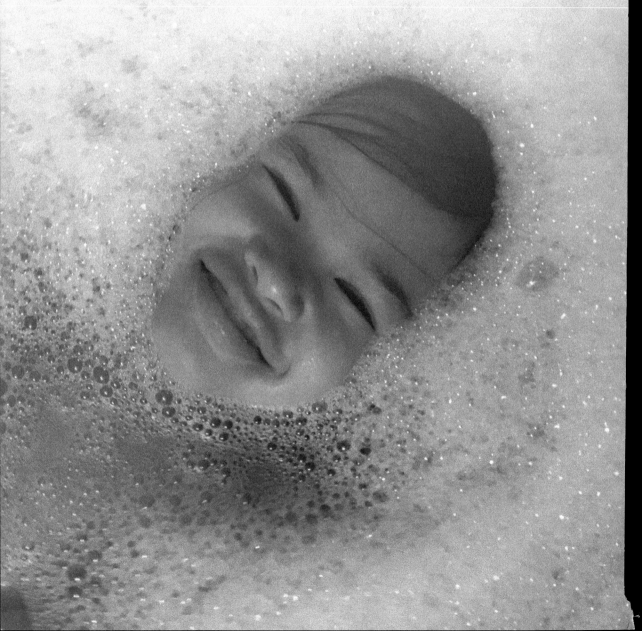